HTML & CS

CODE AND CONQUER

OLIVER LUCAS JR

TABLE OF CONTENTS

Chapter 1

1.1 The Internet & The World Wide Web
1.2 The Role of HTML & CSS
1.3 Setting Up Your Development Environment

Chapter 2

2.1 Basic HTML Structure & Syntax
2.2 Essential HTML Elements (Headings, Paragraphs, Links)
2.3 Working with Text and Images

Chapter 3

3.1 Understanding CSS Syntax and Selectors
3.2 Basic Styling (Colors, Fonts, Backgrounds)

Chapter 4

4.1 Ordered and Unordered Lists
4.2 Creating Tables for Data Organization
4.3 Styling Lists and Tables with CSS

Chapter 5

5.1 Creating Forms with HTML
5.2 Input Types and Attributes
5.3 Styling Forms for Usability and Aesthetics

Chapter 6

6.1 Dividing the Page with <div> Elements
6.2 Creating Navigation Menus
6.3 CSS Layout Techniques (Flexbox, Grid)

Chapter 7

7.1 Understanding Media Queries
7.2 Designing for Different Screen Sizes
7.3 Mobile-First Approach

Chapter 8

8.1 Embedding Images and Videos
8.2 Audio Integration and Control
8.3 Accessibility Considerations

Chapter 9

9.1 Introduction to Popular Frameworks (Bootstrap, Tailwind CSS)
9.2 Using CSS Preprocessors (Sass, Less)
9.3 Streamlining Your Workflow

Chapter 10

10.1 Common HTML and CSS Errors
10.2 Using Browser Developer Tools
10.3 Optimizing for Performance and Accessibility

Preface

Welcome to **HTML & CSS: Code & Conquer**, your guide to mastering the essential languages of the web. Whether you're a complete beginner taking your first steps into the world of web development or an aspiring designer looking to enhance your skills, this book is designed to equip you with the knowledge and confidence to build stunning, interactive websites.

In this book, we'll embark on a journey through the foundations of HTML and CSS. We'll start with the basics, exploring the structure of web pages, essential elements, and fundamental styling techniques. As we progress, we'll delve into more advanced topics like responsive design, multimedia integration, and CSS frameworks, empowering you to create dynamic and engaging web experiences.

This book is more than just a dry technical manual. We believe that learning should be engaging and enjoyable. We've infused the pages with clear explanations, practical examples, and real-world analogies to make complex concepts easy to understand.

Here's what you can expect:

Clear and concise language: We've stripped away jargon and technical complexities to make the content accessible to everyone.

Practical examples: Each chapter is packed with hands-on examples that demonstrate how to apply the concepts in real-world scenarios.

Engaging analogies: We use relatable analogies to explain complex topics, making them easier to grasp and remember.

Step-by-step guidance: We guide you through each concept with clear instructions and helpful tips.

A focus on best practices: We emphasize industry best practices and modern web development techniques.

By the end of this book, you'll have the skills and confidence to:

Build web pages from scratch using HTML.

Style your pages with CSS to create visually appealing designs.

Create responsive websites that adapt to different screen sizes.

Incorporate multimedia elements like images, videos, and audio.

Use CSS frameworks and preprocessors to streamline your workflow.

Debug and optimize your websites for performance and accessibility.

We're excited to join you on this journey of web development discovery. Let's dive in and start coding!

Chapter 1

Welcome to the Web

1.1 The Internet & The World Wide Web

Imagine a vast network of roads connecting cities and towns across the globe. That's essentially what the **Internet** is – a massive network of interconnected computers and servers that spans the entire planet. These connections allow computers to communicate with each other and share information, no matter where they are located.

Now, imagine that along these roads, there are countless libraries, museums, shops, and communities, all filled with information and resources. That's the **World Wide Web**. It's a collection of interconnected documents and other resources, linked together by hyperlinks and accessed through the Internet.

Think of the Internet as the infrastructure – the roads and highways. The World Wide Web is what travels on those roads – the cars, buses, and trucks carrying information and services.

Key Differences:

The Internet is the underlying network that makes it all possible. It's the hardware and infrastructure that allows computers to connect and communicate.

The World Wide Web is a system of interlinked documents and resources accessed through the Internet. It's the software and content that we interact with.

How They Work Together:

When you type a website address (like `www.google.com`) into your browser, your computer uses the Internet to connect to the server where that website is stored. The server then sends the website's files back to your computer through the Internet, and your browser displays them as a web page.

Key Takeaways:

The Internet is the foundation upon which the World Wide Web is built.

The World Wide Web is just one of the many services that run on the Internet (others include email, file sharing, and online gaming).

HTML and CSS are the languages used to create and style the content on the World Wide Web.

By understanding the relationship between the Internet and the World Wide Web, you'll gain a deeper appreciation for how websites work and how you can use HTML and CSS to build your own online presence.

1.2 The Role of HTML & CSS

Now that you understand the difference between the Internet and the World Wide Web, let's explore the two essential languages that make websites possible: HTML and CSS. They work together like a dynamic duo, each with a unique role to play in bringing web pages to life.

HTML: The Architect

Think of HTML (HyperText Markup Language) as the architect of a web page. It provides the structure and content, laying the foundation for everything you see and interact with online. HTML uses a system of tags to define different elements, like headings, paragraphs, images, and links. These tags tell the browser how to organize and display the content on the page.

Imagine building a house:

HTML is like the blueprint that defines the rooms, walls, doors, and windows.

Each HTML tag is like a specific instruction for building a part of the house (e.g., `<p>` for a paragraph, `<h1>` for a main heading).

CSS: The Interior Designer

CSS (Cascading Style Sheets) is the interior designer of the web. It takes the basic structure created by HTML and adds visual style and flair. CSS controls how elements look, including their colors, fonts, sizes, spacing, and positioning.

Back to our house analogy:

CSS is like choosing the paint colors, furniture, decorations, and lighting to make the house look beautiful and inviting.

CSS stylesheets are like the design plans that specify the aesthetic details of each room.

Working Together in Harmony

HTML and CSS work in tandem to create the complete web experience. HTML provides the raw content and structure, while CSS enhances its presentation and visual appeal. This separation of concerns allows for greater flexibility and control in web design.

Key Takeaways:

HTML provides the structure and content of a web page.

controls the visual presentation and styling of a web page.

HTML and CSS are essential for building modern, engaging websites.

By mastering HTML and CSS, you'll have the power to create any website you can imagine. You'll be able to structure content effectively and style it to match your vision, creating a compelling online presence for yourself or your business.

1.3 Setting Up Your Development Environment

Before you embark on your web development journey, you need to set up a comfortable and efficient workspace. Think of it as preparing your artist's studio or your chef's kitchen. A well-organized development environment will make coding smoother, faster, and more enjoyable. Here's what you'll need:

1. A Code Editor

A code editor is your digital canvas. It's where you'll write and edit your HTML and CSS code. Choose an editor that's user-friendly and offers helpful features like syntax highlighting, auto-completion, and error detection. Some popular options include:

VS Code: A free, open-source editor with a vast library of extensions.

Sublime Text: A fast and lightweight editor with a customizable interface.

Atom: A hackable editor developed by GitHub with a strong community.

Notepad++: A simple and free editor for Windows users.

2. A Web Browser

You'll need a web browser to view your web pages and test your code. Popular choices include:

Google Chrome: Known for its developer tools and fast performance.

Mozilla Firefox: A privacy-focused browser with excellent developer tools.

Microsoft Edge: A modern browser based on Chromium with good compatibility.

Safari: Apple's browser, essential for testing on Apple devices.

3. A File Management System

Organize your website files and folders in a clear and logical way. Create a dedicated folder for your project and use subfolders for different types of files (HTML, CSS, images).

4. Basic Understanding of Files and Folders

Familiarize yourself with how files and folders work on your computer. Learn how to create, rename, move, and delete files and folders.

5. (Optional) A Local Server

While not strictly necessary for beginners, a local server can be helpful for testing more advanced features. It simulates a live web server on your computer.

Setting Up Your Editor

Once you've chosen a code editor, take some time to explore its features and customize it to your preferences. Here are some tips:

Install helpful extensions: Many editors offer extensions that can enhance your workflow, such as linters (for code quality), formatters (for consistent code style), and Emmet (for faster HTML writing).

Customize the theme: Choose a color scheme that's easy on your eyes and helps you focus.

Configure keyboard shortcuts: Learn the shortcuts for common actions to speed up your coding.

Ready to Code

With your development environment set up, you're ready to start writing HTML and CSS code! In the next chapter, we'll dive into the basics of HTML and learn how to create your first web page.

Chapter 2

HTML Essentials

2.1 Basic HTML Structure & Syntax

Let's begin constructing our web pages! Just as a house needs a solid framework, every HTML document follows a specific structure. This structure ensures that web browsers can understand and display your content correctly.

The Basic Skeleton

Every HTML document has the following essential elements:

HTML

```
<!DOCTYPE html>
<html lang="en">
<head>
  <meta charset="UTF-8">
  <title>My First Web Page</title>
</head>
<body>

  </body>
</html>
```

Let's break down each part:

`<!DOCTYPE html>`: This declaration tells the browser that we're using the latest version of HTML (HTML5).

`<html lang="en">`: This tag marks the beginning of the HTML document and specifies the language as English (`en`).

`<head>`: This section contains metadata about the page, such as the title and character set. It doesn't appear directly on the page itself.

`<meta charset="UTF-8">`: This tag specifies the character encoding, ensuring that your page displays characters correctly.

`<title>My First Web Page</title>`: This tag sets the title that appears in the browser tab or window title bar.

`<body>`: This section contains the content that will be displayed on the web page, such as text, images, and links.

HTML Syntax: Tags and Elements

HTML uses **tags** to define elements. Tags are keywords enclosed in angle brackets (< and >). Most tags come in pairs: an opening tag (`<tag>`) and a closing tag (`</tag>`). The content between the opening and closing tags is the element's content.

For example:

HTML

```
<p>This is a paragraph of text.</p>
```

`<p>` is the opening tag.

`</p>` is the closing tag.

"This is a paragraph of text." is the content of the paragraph element.

Important Notes:

Case-insensitivity: HTML tags are not case-sensitive, but it's good practice to use lowercase.

Nesting: Elements can be nested inside other elements to create hierarchy and structure.

Attributes: Tags can have attributes that provide additional information about the element. Attributes are written within the opening tag and follow the format `attribute="value"`.

Example:

HTML

```
<a               href="https://www.example.com"
target="_blank">This is a link</a>
```

In this example, the `<a>` tag (for a hyperlink) has two attributes:

`href`: Specifies the URL the link points to.

`target`: Specifies where the link should open (in this case, a new tab).

By understanding this basic structure and syntax, you're well on your way to writing valid and well-formed HTML code. In the next section, we'll explore some essential HTML elements that you'll use to build your web pages.

2.2 Essential HTML Elements (Headings, Paragraphs, Links)

Now that you know the basic structure of an HTML document, let's explore some of the most common elements you'll use to add content to your web pages.

Headings

Headings are used to organize your content and create a hierarchy of information. HTML provides six levels of headings, from `<h1>` (the most important) to `<h6>` (the least important).

HTML

```
<h1>This is a main heading</h1>
<h2>This is a subheading</h2>
<h3>This is a smaller subheading</h3>
```

Paragraphs

Paragraphs are used to group blocks of text. The `<p>` tag defines a paragraph.

HTML

```
<p>This is a paragraph of text. It can contain
multiple sentences and lines.</p>
<p>This is another paragraph.</p>
```

Links

Links (or hyperlinks) allow users to navigate between different web pages or resources. The `<a>` tag (anchor tag) creates a link. The `href` attribute specifies the URL (web address) that the link points to.

HTML

```html
<a href="https://www.google.com">Go to Google</a>
```

This code will create a link that says "Go to Google" and takes the user to the Google homepage when clicked.

Putting it Together

Here's an example of how you can use these elements to create a simple web page:

HTML

```html
<!DOCTYPE html>
<html lang="en">
<head>
  <meta charset="UTF-8">
  <title>My First Web Page</title>
</head>
<body>
```

```html
<h1>Welcome to My Website!</h1>

    <p>This is my first web page. I'm excited to
learn HTML and CSS.</p>


        <a    href="https://www.example.com">Learn
more</a>


</body>

</html>
```

This code will create a web page with a main heading, a paragraph of text, and a link to another website.

Key Takeaways:

Use headings to structure your content and create a hierarchy of information.

Use paragraphs to group related text together.

Use links to connect your web pages and provide access to other resources.

By mastering these essential HTML elements, you can start creating web pages with structured content and basic navigation. In the next section, we'll explore how to work with text and images to add more variety to your pages.

2.3 Working with Text and Images

HTML provides a variety of elements for formatting text and adding images to your web pages. Let's explore some of the most common ones:

Formatting Text

Line Breaks: The `<br>` tag inserts a single line break.

HTML

```
<p>This is the first line.<br>This is the second
line.</p>
```

Strong and Emphasis: The `<strong>` tag makes text bold, indicating strong importance. The `<em>` tag italicizes text for emphasis.

HTML

```
<p>This is <strong>important</strong> text. This
text is <em>emphasized</em>.</p>
```

Preformatted Text: The `<pre>` tag displays text in a fixed-width font, preserving spaces and line breaks. This is useful for displaying code or poetry.

HTML

```
<pre>
This is
preformatted
text.
</pre>
```

Adding Images

The `<img>` tag is used to embed images in your web page. It requires the `src` attribute to specify the image file's URL or path.

HTML

```
<img src="images/my-image.jpg" alt="A descriptive
alt text">
```

`src`: The URL or path to the image file.

`alt`: Provides alternative text that describes the image. This is important for accessibility (screen readers) and if the image fails to load.

Tips for Working with Images

File Formats: Use common image formats like JPEG, PNG, or GIF.

Optimization: Optimize your images to reduce file size and improve page load speed.

Responsive Images: Use the `srcset` attribute to provide different image sources for different screen sizes.

Accessibility: Always provide descriptive alt text for your images.

Example

HTML

```
<!DOCTYPE html>
<html lang="en">
<head>
  <meta charset="UTF-8">
  <title>Text and Images</title>
</head>
<body>


  <h1>Working with Text and Images</h1>


    <p>This    is    a    paragraph    with    a
<strong>bold</strong>        word        and        an
<em>italicized</em> word.</p>


  <img src="images/my-image.jpg" alt="A beautiful
landscape">


</body>
</html>
```

This code will display a heading, a paragraph with formatted text, and an image.

Key Takeaways:

HTML provides elements for formatting text and adding images to your web pages.

Use the `<img>` tag to embed images and always include descriptive alt text.

Optimize your images for web use to improve page load speed.

By combining text formatting and images, you can create engaging and visually appealing web pages. In the next chapter, we'll delve deeper into CSS and learn how to style these elements.

Chapter 3

Introduction to CSS

3.1 Understanding CSS Syntax and Selectors

Now it's time to add some style! CSS (Cascading Style Sheets) is the language we use to make our web pages visually appealing. To effectively use CSS, you need to understand its syntax and how to target specific HTML elements with selectors.

CSS Syntax: The Rule of Style

CSS code is composed of **rules**. Each rule has two main parts:

Selector: This specifies which HTML element(s) you want to style.

Declaration Block: This contains one or more declarations that define the styles you want to apply.

Here's the basic structure of a CSS rule:

CSS

```css
selector {
   property1: value1;
   property2: value2;
   property3: value3;
}
```

Selector: Points to the HTML element you want to style (e.g., p, h1, div).

Declaration: Consists of a property (e.g., `color`, `font-size`) and a value (e.g., `blue`, `16px`) separated by a colon.

Property: A specific style attribute you want to change (e.g., the color of the text).

Value: The value you want to assign to the property.

Declaration Block: Enclosed in curly braces { }, it contains one or more declarations separated by semicolons.

Example:

CSS

```
p {
  color: blue;
  font-size: 16px;
}
```

This CSS rule will make all paragraphs on your page have blue text with a font size of 16 pixels.

CSS Selectors: Targeting Elements

Selectors are the key to applying styles precisely where you want them. Here are some common types of selectors:

Element Selector: Targets all elements of a specific type.

CSS

```
p { /* Styles all paragraph elements */ }
h1 { /* Styles all h1 heading elements */ }
```

Class Selector: Targets elements with a specific class attribute. You define classes in your HTML using the `class` attribute.

HTML

```
<p    class="highlight">This    paragraph    is
highlighted.</p>
```

CSS

```
.highlight  {  /*  Styles  all  elements  with  the
class "highlight" */ }
```

ID Selector: Targets a single element with a specific ID attribute. IDs should be unique within an HTML document.

HTML

```
<h1   id="main-heading">This    is    the    main
heading</h1>
```

CSS

```
#main-heading { /* Styles the element with the ID
"main-heading" */ }
```

Key Takeaways:

CSS uses rules to define styles for HTML elements.

Selectors identify which elements to style.

Declarations specify the styles to be applied.

By understanding CSS syntax and selectors, you can begin to control the appearance of your web pages with precision. In the next section, we'll explore some basic styling properties to change the look of your text, backgrounds, and more.

3.2 Basic Styling (Colors, Fonts, Backgrounds)

Let's dive into some essential CSS properties that allow you to control the visual presentation of your web page elements.

Colors

CSS offers several ways to specify colors:

Color Names: Use predefined color names like red, blue, green, black, white, etc.

CSS

```
p {
    color: blue;
```

```
}
```

Hexadecimal Codes: Use a six-digit hexadecimal code (e.g., `#FF0000` for red) to represent colors.

CSS

```css
h1 {
  color: #008000; /* Green */
}
```

RGB Values: Specify colors using red, green, and blue values (e.g., `rgb(255, 0, 0)` for red).

CSS

```css
a {
  color: rgb(0, 0, 255); /* Blue */
}
```

Fonts

`font-family`: Sets the font for an element. You can specify a specific font (e.g., "Arial") or a generic font family (e.g., "sans-serif").

CSS

```
body {
    font-family: Arial, sans-serif;
}
```

`font-size`: Sets the size of the font. You can use units like pixels (`px`), ems (`em`), or percentages (`%`).

CSS

```
h2 {
    font-size: 24px;
}
```

`font-weight`: Sets the boldness of the font. Common values include `normal`, `bold`, and numerical values (e.g., `400` for normal, `700` for bold).

CSS

```css
strong {
  font-weight: bold;
}
```

font-style: Sets the style of the font, such as normal, italic, or oblique.

CSS

```css
em {
  font-style: italic;
}
```

Backgrounds

background-color: Sets the background color of an element.

CSS

```css
body {
  background-color: #f0f0f0; /* Light gray */
}
```

`background-image`: Sets a background image for an element.

CSS

```
div {
  background-image: url("images/background.jpg");
}
```

`background-repeat`: Controls how the background image repeats (e.g., repeat, repeat-x, repeat-y, no-repeat).

`background-position`: Specifies the position of the background image (e.g., center, top left, bottom right).

Example

CSS

```
body {
  font-family: Georgia, serif;
  background-color: #f4f4f4;
}


h1 {
  color: #333;
  font-size: 36px;
}
```

```
p {
    color: #666;
    line-height: 1.5;
}
```

This CSS code will style the entire page with a Georgia font and a light gray background. Headings will be dark gray and large, while paragraphs will have a slightly lighter gray color and increased line spacing.

Key Takeaways:

CSS provides properties to control colors, fonts, and backgrounds.

You can specify colors using names, hexadecimal codes, or RGB values.

Use font properties to adjust the font family, size, weight, and style.

Background properties allow you to set background colors and images.

By experimenting with these basic styling properties, you can start transforming the look and feel of your web pages. In the next section, we'll explore the box model, a fundamental concept in CSS that governs how elements are laid out on the page.

Chapter 4

Working with Lists and Tables

4.1 Ordered and Unordered Lists

Lists are essential for organizing information on web pages. HTML provides two main types of lists: ordered and unordered.

Unordered Lists (`<ul>`): For Items Without a Specific Order

Unordered lists are used when the order of the items doesn't matter. They are typically displayed with bullet points.

`<ul>`: The unordered list tag.

`<li>`: The list item tag (placed inside `<ul>`).

Example:

HTML

```
<ul>
  <li>Apples</li>
  <li>Bananas</li>
  <li>Oranges</li>
</ul>
```

This code will create a bulleted list of fruits:

Apples

Bananas

Oranges

Ordered Lists (`<ol>`): For Sequential Information

Ordered lists are used when the order of the items is important. They are typically displayed with numbers or letters.

`<ol>`: The ordered list tag.

`<li>`: The list item tag (placed inside `<ol>`).

Example:

HTML

```
<ol>
   <li>Preheat the oven.</li>
   <li>Mix the ingredients.</li>
   <li>Bake for 30 minutes.</li>
</ol>
```

This code will create a numbered list of baking instructions:

Preheat the oven.

Mix the ingredients.

Bake for 30 minutes.

Nesting Lists

You can create nested lists by placing a list inside another list item. This is useful for creating hierarchical structures.

Example:

HTML

```
<ul>
  <li>Fruits
    <ul>
      <li>Apples</li>
      <li>Bananas</li>
    </ul>
  </li>
  <li>Vegetables
    <ul>
      <li>Carrots</li>
      <li>Broccoli</li>
    </ul>
  </li>
</ul>
```

This code will create a nested list of fruits and vegetables.

Key Takeaways:

Use unordered lists (`<ul>`) for items without a specific order.

Use ordered lists (`<ol>`) for sequential information.

You can nest lists to create hierarchical structures.

In the next section, we'll learn how to create tables for organizing data in rows and columns.

4.2 Creating Tables for Data Organization

Tables are a powerful tool for presenting structured data in a clear and organized way. They are made up of rows and columns, forming a grid-like structure. HTML provides a set of elements specifically designed for creating tables.

Basic Table Structure

`<table>`: The table tag, which defines the entire table.

`<tr>`: The table row tag, which defines a row in the table.

`<td>`: The table data tag, which defines a cell in a row that contains data.

`<th>`: The table header tag, which defines a cell in a row that acts as a header for a column.

Example:

HTML

```
<table>
  <tr>
    <th>Name</th>
    <th>Age</th>
    <th>City</th>
  </tr>
  <tr>
    <td>John Doe</td>
    <td>30</td>
```

```
    <td>New York</td>
  </tr>
  <tr>
    <td>Jane Smith</td>
    <td>25</td>
    <td>Los Angeles</td>
  </tr>
</table>
```
[1]

This code will create a simple table with three columns (Name, Age, City) and two rows of data.

Adding Structure with `<thead>`**,** `<tbody>`**, and** `<tfoot>`

For larger tables, you can improve readability and structure by using the following tags:

`<thead>`: Groups the header rows of the table.

`<tbody>`: Groups the body rows of the table (the data).

`<tfoot>`: Groups the footer rows of the table (optional, for summary information).

Example:

HTML

```
<table>
  <thead>
    <tr>
      <th>Name</th>
```

```
      <th>Age</th>
      <th>City</th>
    </tr>
  </thead>
  <tbody>
    <tr>
      <td>John Doe</td>
      <td>30</td>
      <td>New York</td>
    </tr>
    <tr>
      <td>Jane Smith</td>
      <td>25</td>
      <td>Los Angeles</td>
    </tr>²
  </tbody>
</table>
```

Spanning Rows and Columns

You can make cells span across multiple rows or columns using the `rowspan` and `colspan` attributes in the `<td>` or `<th>` tags.

Example:

HTML

```
<tr>
```

```
<th colspan="2">Contact Information</th>
</tr>
```

This will make the "Contact Information" header span across two columns.

Key Takeaways:

Tables are created using the `<table>`, `<tr>`, `<td>`, and `<th>` tags.

Use `<thead>`, `<tbody>`, and `<tfoot>` to structure larger tables.

You can use `rowspan` and `colspan` to make cells span multiple rows or columns.

By understanding how to create and structure tables, you can effectively organize and present data on your web pages. In the next section, we'll explore how to style lists and tables with CSS to enhance their visual appearance.

4.3 Styling Lists and Tables with CSS

CSS provides a wide range of properties for styling lists and tables, allowing you to customize their appearance to match your website's design.

Styling Lists

`list-style-type`: Changes the bullet style for unordered lists (e.g., `disc`, `circle`, `square`, `none`).

CSS

```
ul {
```

```
    list-style-type: circle;
}
```

list-style-position: Controls the position of the bullet or number (e.g., inside, outside).

CSS

```
ul {
    list-style-position: inside;
}
```

list-style-image: Uses an image as the list marker.

CSS

```
ul {
    list-style-image: url('images/star.png');
}
```

Other styling: You can apply other CSS properties to lists and list items, such as color, font-size, margin, padding, and background-color.

Styling Tables

`border-collapse`: Controls the borders between table cells (e.g., `collapse` to merge borders, `separate` for distinct borders).

CSS

```
table {
  border-collapse: collapse;
}
```

`border`: Sets the border style, width, and color for table elements.

CSS

```
table, th, td {
  border: 1px solid black;
}
```

`padding`: Adds space between the cell content and the cell border.

CSS

```css
td {
    padding: 10px;
}
```

text-align: Aligns the text within table cells (e.g., left, center, right).

vertical-align: Aligns the content vertically within table cells (e.g., top, middle, bottom).

background-color: Sets the background color of table cells.

:hover: Applies styles when the user hovers over a table row.

Example: Styling a Table

CSS

```css
table {
    width: 80%;
    margin: 20px auto;
    border-collapse: collapse;
}

th, td {
    border: 1px solid #ddd;
```

```css
  padding: 8px;

  text-align: left;

}


th {

  background-color:[1] #f0f0f0;

}


tr:nth-child(even) {

  background-color: #f2f2f2;[2]

}


tr:hover {

  background-color: #ddd;

}
```

This CSS code styles a table with borders, padding, alternating row colors, and a hover effect.

Key Takeaways:

CSS provides properties to customize the appearance of lists and tables.

You can change the bullet style, position, and image for lists.

Tables can be styled with borders, padding, text alignment, and background colors.

By applying CSS styles to lists and tables, you can enhance their visual presentation and make them more engaging and user-friendly. In the next chapter, we'll move on to forms and user input, learning how to create interactive elements on your web pages.

Chapter 5

Forms and User Input

5.1 Creating Forms with HTML

It seems like you might want to revisit the topic of creating forms in HTML. That's perfectly fine! It's an important part of web development, and it's good to make sure you have a solid understanding.

To recap the key concepts from our previous discussion:

The `<form>` Element:

This is the container that holds all the elements of your form. Think of it like the frame of a picture.

It has attributes like `action` (where the form data is sent) and `method` (how the data is sent - usually `get` or `post`).

Form Controls:

These are the individual elements within a form that allow users to interact and provide input.

`<input>`: This is a versatile element with many types:

`type="text"`: For single-line text input.

`type="password"`: For passwords (hides the characters).

`type="email"`: For email addresses.

`type="number"`: For numbers.

`type="submit"`: Creates the submit button.

`<textarea>`: For multi-line text input (like a comment box).

`<select>`: Creates a dropdown list.

`<option>`: Defines the individual options in the dropdown.

`<button>`: Creates a clickable button.

`<label>`: Provides a label for a form control (important for accessibility).

`<fieldset>`: Groups related form elements together.

`<legend>`: Provides a caption for a `<fieldset>`.

Example:

HTML

```
<form action="/process_data" method="post">
  <label for="username">Username:</label>
       <input     type="text"     id="username"
name="username"><br><br>


  <label for="password">Password:</label>
     <input    type="password"    id="password"
name="password"><br><br>


  <input type="submit" value="Login">[1]
</form>
```

This code creates a simple login form with fields for username and password.

Do you have any specific questions about creating forms with HTML? For example, maybe you'd like to know:

How to use different input types?

How to style forms with CSS?

How to validate form data?

How to handle form submissions with server-side code?

I'm here to help you understand any aspect of HTML forms that you're curious about! Just let me know what you'd like to learn more about.

5.2 Input Types and Attributes

The `<input>` element is incredibly versatile thanks to its `type` attribute, which determines the kind of input it accepts. Let's explore some common input types and their attributes:

Common Input Types

`text`: For single-line text input (default).

HTML

```
<input          type="text"          name="username"
placeholder="Enter your username">
```

`password`: For passwords (characters are masked).

HTML

```
<input type="password" name="password">
```

email: For email addresses (some browsers perform basic validation).

HTML

```
<input type="email" name="email">
```

number: For numeric input (may include attributes like min and max).

HTML

```
<input type="number" name="age" min="18" max="120">
```

date: For selecting dates.

HTML

```
<input type="date" name="birthday">
```

`checkbox`: For selecting one or more options from a set.

HTML

```
<input          type="checkbox"          name="hobbies"
value="reading"> Reading
```

```
<input          type="checkbox"          name="hobbies"
value="coding"> Coding
```

`radio`: For selecting a single option from a set (use the same `name` attribute for related radio buttons).

HTML

```
<input  type="radio"  name="gender"  value="male">
Male
```

```
<input type="radio" name="gender" value="female">
Female
```

`submit`: Creates a submit button to send the form data.

HTML

```
<input type="submit" value="Submit">
```

`file`: Allows users to upload files.

HTML

```
<input type="file" name="profile_picture">
```

Common Input Attributes

`name`: Gives the input field a name, which is used to identify the data when the form is submitted.

`value`: Sets the initial value of the input field.

`placeholder`: Provides a hint or example text inside the input field.

`required`: Makes the input field mandatory.

`readonly`: Prevents the user from editing the input field.

`disabled`: Disables the input field (it cannot be interacted with or submitted).

Example: Using Attributes

HTML

```
<label for="email">Email:</label>

<input    type="email"    id="email"    name="email"
placeholder="yourname@example.com" required>
```

This code creates an email input field with a label, a placeholder, and makes it a required field.

Key Takeaways:

The `type` attribute determines the behavior and appearance of an `<input>` element.

Input fields can have various attributes to control their functionality and appearance.

Use attributes like `placeholder` and `required` to improve usability and guide users.

By understanding different input types and attributes, you can create versatile and user-friendly forms that collect the information you need. In the next section, we'll explore how to style forms with CSS to enhance their visual appeal and integrate them seamlessly into your website's design.

5.3 Styling Forms for Usability and Aesthetics

While HTML provides the structure for forms, CSS empowers you to enhance their visual appeal and improve their usability. By styling form elements, you can create a more engaging and user-friendly experience.

General Form Styling

Layout: Use CSS properties like `display` (e.g., `block`, `inline-block`, `flex`, `grid`), `width`, `margin`, and `padding` to arrange form elements in a clear and logical way. Consider using a grid system for complex layouts.

Typography: Choose legible fonts and appropriate font sizes for labels and input fields. Ensure sufficient color contrast for readability.

Spacing: Use whitespace effectively to create visual separation between form elements and improve readability.

Borders and Shadows: Apply borders and box shadows to define input fields and create visual depth.

Styling Specific Elements

Labels: Style labels to be clear and descriptive. Use `font-weight`, `color`, and `position` to make them stand out.

Input Fields: Style input fields with `border`, `padding`, `background-color`, `font-size`, and `color`. Consider using the `:focus` pseudo-class to provide visual feedback when a field is selected.

Buttons: Make buttons visually prominent and inviting. Use `background-color`, `color`, `border`, `padding`, and `cursor: pointer` to style them. Consider using the `:hover` pseudo-class to provide visual feedback on mouse hover.

Error Messages: Style error messages to be noticeable but not overly intrusive. Use colors and icons to indicate errors clearly.

Usability Considerations

Focus States: Provide clear visual cues when an element is in focus (e.g., using a different border color or outline).

Disabled States: Style disabled elements to indicate that they cannot be interacted with.

Error Handling: Provide clear and concise error messages to guide users.

Accessibility: Ensure sufficient color contrast and use ARIA attributes to improve accessibility for users with disabilities.

Example: Styling a Submit Button

CSS

```
input[type="submit"] {
    background-color: #007bff; /* Blue background */
  color: white;
  padding: 10px 20px;
  border: none;
  cursor: pointer;
}


input[type="submit"]:hover {
    background-color: #0069d9; /* Darker blue on hover */
  }
```

This CSS code styles a submit button with a blue background, white text, padding, and a hover effect.

Key Takeaways:

CSS is crucial for enhancing the usability and aesthetics of forms.

Consider layout, typography, spacing, and visual cues when styling forms.

Style specific elements like labels, input fields, and buttons to create a consistent and user-friendly experience.

Always keep accessibility in mind when styling forms.

By combining HTML for structure and CSS for styling, you can create visually appealing and user-friendly forms that enhance the overall experience of your website. In the next chapter, we'll move on to layout and navigation, exploring how to structure the content on your web pages.

Chapter 6

Layout and Navigation

6.1 Dividing the Page with `<div>` Elements

The `<div>` element is a fundamental building block for creating web page layouts. It acts as a container that groups and structures other HTML elements. By strategically using `<div>` elements, you can divide your page into distinct sections, such as headers, footers, sidebars, and main content areas.

The `<div>` Tag: A Versatile Container

The `<div>` tag itself doesn't have any inherent visual styling. It's a semantic element that provides a way to organize your content. You can then use CSS to style and position these `<div>` containers to create your desired layout.

Example: Basic Page Structure

HTML

```
<div id="header">

  <h1>My Website</h1>

  <nav>

    </nav>

</div>


<div id="main">

  <div id="sidebar">
```

```html
  </div>
  <div id="content">
  </div>
</div>


<div id="footer">
  <p>&copy; 2024 My Website</p>
</div>
```

In this example, we've divided the page into three main sections:

`header`: Contains the website title and navigation.

`main`: Contains the main content and a sidebar.

`footer`: Contains the copyright information.

Using Classes for Common Styles

You can use CSS classes to apply the same styles to multiple `<div>` elements. This promotes consistency and reduces code duplication.

Example:

HTML

```html
<div class="container">
  </div>


<div class="container">
  </div>
```

CSS

```css
.container {
  width: 80%;
  margin: 0 auto;
  padding: 20px;
}
```

This CSS code will apply the same styles (width, margin, padding) to both `<div>` elements with the class "container."

Key Takeaways:

The `<div>` element is a versatile container for structuring web page content.

Use `<div>` elements to divide your page into logical sections.

Combine `<div>` elements with CSS to create various layouts.

Use CSS classes to apply common styles to multiple `<div>` elements.

By mastering the use of `<div>` elements and CSS, you can create complex and visually appealing layouts for your web pages. In the next section, we'll explore how to create navigation menus using lists and links.

6.2 Creating Navigation Menus

Navigation menus are crucial for helping users find their way around your website. They provide a structured list of links to different sections or pages, making it easy for users to explore your content. HTML lists (`<ul>` or `<ol>`) combined with links (`<a>`) are the foundation for creating navigation menus.

Basic Navigation Structure

HTML

```
<nav>
  <ul>
    <li><a href="index.html">Home</a></li>
    <li><a href="about.html">About</a></li>
    <li><a href="services.html">Services</a></li>
    <li><a href="contact.html">Contact</a></li>
  </ul>
</nav>
```

This code creates a simple navigation menu with links to four pages: Home, About, Services, and Contact. The `<nav>` element provides semantic meaning, indicating that this is a navigation section.

Styling with CSS

CSS is essential for making your navigation menu visually appealing and functional. Here are some common styling techniques:

Remove bullet points:

CSS

```css
nav ul {
  list-style-type: none;
  margin: 0;
  padding: 0;
}
```

Horizontal menu:

CSS

```css
nav ul {
    display: flex;  /* Use Flexbox for easy
horizontal layout */
}


nav li {
  margin-right: 20px;
}
```

Hover effects:

CSS

```css
nav a:hover {
```

```
  text-decoration: underline;

  color: blue;

}
```

Active state:

CSS

```
nav a.active {

  font-weight: bold;

}
```

(You'll need to add the `class="active"` attribute to the `<a>` tag of the currently active page)

Advanced Navigation

Dropdown menus: Create nested lists (`<ul>`) within list items (`<li>`) to create dropdown menus. Use CSS to control their visibility and behavior.

Responsive menus: Use media queries in CSS to adapt the menu layout for different screen sizes (e.g., creating a hamburger menu for mobile devices).

JavaScript enhancements: Use JavaScript to add interactive features like smooth scrolling or animated transitions.

Key Takeaways:

Use lists (`<ul>` or `<ol>`) and links (`<a>`) to create navigation menus.

The `<nav>` element provides semantic meaning for navigation sections.

CSS is essential for styling and positioning menu items.

Consider using advanced techniques like dropdown menus and responsive design to enhance your navigation.

By combining HTML structure with CSS styling, you can create user-friendly and visually appealing navigation menus that improve the overall experience on your website. In the next section, we'll delve into CSS layout techniques, exploring how to arrange content on your pages effectively.

6.3 CSS Layout Techniques (Flexbox, Grid)

CSS offers powerful layout techniques like Flexbox and Grid, which provide greater control and flexibility in arranging elements on your web pages. These methods have revolutionized web design, making it easier to create complex and responsive layouts.

Flexbox: The Flexible Box Module

Flexbox is a one-dimensional layout model that excels at aligning and distributing elements along a single axis (either a row or a column). It's ideal for:

Centering elements both vertically and horizontally.

Creating flexible layouts that adapt to different screen sizes.

Distributing space between elements.

Reordering elements without changing the HTML structure.

Key Flexbox Properties

`display: flex;`: Applies Flexbox to a container element.

`flex-direction`: Sets the direction of the main axis (e.g., `row`, `column`).

`justify-content`: Aligns items along the main axis (e.g., `center`, `space-between`, `space-around`).

`align-items`: Aligns items along the cross axis (e.g., `center`, `flex-start`, `flex-end`).

`flex-wrap`: Controls whether items wrap onto multiple lines (e.g., `wrap`, `nowrap`).

`flex-grow`, `flex-shrink`, `flex-basis`: Control how items grow or shrink to fill available space.

Grid: The Two-Dimensional Layout System

CSS Grid is a two-dimensional layout system that allows you to arrange elements into rows and columns. It's ideal for:

Creating complex grid-based layouts.

Controlling the placement of elements across rows and columns.

Overlapping elements.

Creating responsive layouts that adapt to different screen sizes.

Key Grid Properties

`display: grid;`: Applies Grid layout to a container element.

`grid-template-columns`: Defines the number and size of columns.

`grid-template-rows`: Defines the number and size of rows.

`grid-gap`: Sets the spacing between rows and columns.

`grid-column`, `grid-row`: Control the placement of individual items within the grid.

`grid-template-areas`: Defines named grid areas for easier layout.

Choosing Between Flexbox and Grid

Use Flexbox for one-dimensional layouts (rows or columns).

Use Grid for two-dimensional layouts (rows and columns).

Often, you can combine Flexbox and Grid to achieve complex layouts.

Key Takeaways:

Flexbox and Grid are powerful CSS layout techniques.

Flexbox excels at one-dimensional layouts and element alignment.

Grid excels at two-dimensional layouts and precise element placement.

Choose the appropriate technique based on your layout needs.

By mastering Flexbox and Grid, you can create sophisticated and responsive web layouts with ease. In the next chapter, we'll explore responsive web design, learning how to make your websites adapt to different screen sizes.

Chapter 7

Responsive Web Design

7.1 Understanding Media Queries

Media queries are a cornerstone of responsive web design. They allow you to apply different CSS styles based on characteristics of the user's device, such as screen size, orientation, resolution, and more. This enables you to create websites that adapt seamlessly to various devices, providing an optimal viewing experience for everyone.

The `@media` **Rule**

Media queries use the `@media` rule in CSS to conditionally apply styles. The basic syntax is:

CSS

```css
@media (condition) {
    /* CSS rules to apply when the condition
is met */

}
```

Conditions and Media Features

The `condition` inside the parentheses specifies the criteria for applying the styles. It's composed of media features, which describe specific characteristics of the device or environment. Some common media features include:

`width`: The width of the viewport (browser window).

`height`: The height of the viewport.

`orientation`: The orientation of the device (portrait or landscape).

`max-width`: Applies styles when the viewport width is *below* a certain value.

`min-width`: Applies styles when the viewport width is *above* a certain value.

`resolution`: The pixel density of the screen.

Example: Responsive Layout

CSS

```
/* Default styles for larger screens */
.container {
  width: 960px;
  margin: 0 auto;
}


/* Styles for smaller screens */
@media (max-width: 768px) {
  .container {
```

```
width: 100%;

padding: 20px;

  }

}
```

In this example, the `.container` will have a fixed width of 960px on larger screens. However, on screens with a width of 768px or less, it will take up the full width of the viewport and include padding.

Logical Operators

You can combine multiple media features using logical operators:

`and`: All conditions must be true.

CSS

```
@media (min-width: 768px) and (max-width:
1024px) { ... }
```

`or`: At least one condition must be true (use commas to separate).

CSS

```
@media (max-width: 768px), (orientation:
landscape) { ... }
```

`not`: Negates a condition.

CSS

```
@media not (min-width: 768px) { ... }
```

Key Takeaways:

Media queries allow you to apply different CSS styles based on device characteristics.

The `@media` rule is used to define media queries.

Media features describe specific characteristics like screen size, orientation, and resolution.

You can combine media features using logical operators.

By understanding media queries, you can create websites that adapt to different screen sizes and provide an optimal viewing experience for all users. In the next section, we'll explore how to design for different screen sizes, considering mobile-first and desktop-first approaches.

7.2 Designing for Different Screen Sizes

Responsive web design is about creating websites that adapt gracefully to various screen sizes, from small mobile phones to large desktop monitors. This involves not only using media queries but also adopting a design approach that prioritizes flexibility and adaptability.

Mobile-First vs. Desktop-First

There are two main approaches to responsive design:

Mobile-First: Start by designing for the smallest screen size (mobile) and then progressively enhance the design for larger screens using media queries. This approach prioritizes content and ensures a good experience on mobile devices, which are increasingly dominant.

Desktop-First: Start by designing for the largest screen size (desktop) and then use media queries to adapt the design for smaller screens. This approach can be useful if your website has complex functionality that is primarily used on desktops.

Choosing the Right Approach

The best approach depends on your website's content, target audience, and goals. If mobile usage is a priority, mobile-first is generally recommended. However, if your website is heavily reliant on desktop features, desktop-first might be more suitable.

Key Considerations for Different Screen Sizes

Content Prioritization: Identify the most important content and ensure it's prominently displayed on all screen sizes. Consider rearranging or hiding less important content on smaller screens.

Navigation: Adapt your navigation menu for smaller screens, potentially using a hamburger menu or off-canvas navigation.

Images and Media: Use responsive images to serve appropriately sized images for different screen sizes. Optimize images to reduce file size and improve loading speed.

Typography: Adjust font sizes and line heights to ensure readability on different screen sizes.

Layout: Use flexible layouts that adapt to different screen widths. Consider using CSS Grid or Flexbox for creating responsive grids.

Touch Targets: Ensure that buttons and links are large enough and spaced appropriately for touch interactions on mobile devices.

Testing and Iteration

Thorough testing is essential to ensure your website works well on different screen sizes. Use browser developer tools to simulate various devices, and test on real devices whenever possible. Iterate on your design based on testing feedback to create a truly responsive and user-friendly experience.

Key Takeaways:

Consider both mobile-first and desktop-first approaches, choosing the one that best suits your website's needs.

Prioritize content and adapt navigation for different screen sizes.

Use responsive images and optimize for performance.

Adjust typography and layout to ensure readability and usability.

Test thoroughly on various devices and iterate on your design.

By following these principles, you can create websites that adapt seamlessly to different screen sizes, providing an optimal experience for all users. In the next section, we'll discuss the mobile-first approach in more detail, exploring its benefits and best practices.

7.3 Mobile-First Approach

The mobile-first approach has become a best practice in responsive web design. It involves starting your design process with the smallest screen size (mobile) and then progressively enhancing the design for larger screens using media queries. This approach offers several benefits:

Benefits of Mobile-First

Improved Mobile Experience: By prioritizing mobile users, you ensure that your website is optimized for the devices that are increasingly used to access the web. This leads to better usability, faster loading times, and a more enjoyable experience for mobile users.

Content Prioritization: Starting with a limited screen size forces you to focus on the most essential content and features. This helps you create a streamlined and efficient user experience, avoiding unnecessary clutter.

Performance Optimization: Mobile-first encourages you to start with a lean and efficient codebase, which improves website performance across all devices.

SEO Benefits: Search engines prioritize mobile-friendly websites. By adopting a mobile-first approach, you improve your website's chances of ranking higher in search results.

Easier Maintenance: Starting with a simple mobile design and progressively enhancing it for larger screens makes it easier to maintain and update your website in the long run.

Implementing Mobile-First

Start with the Basics: Begin by creating a basic HTML structure and styling it for mobile devices. Use a viewport meta tag to ensure proper scaling:

HTML

```
<meta                        name="viewport"
content="width=device-width,
initial-scale=1.0">
```

Focus on Content: Prioritize the most important content and features for mobile users. Consider using a single-column layout and simplifying navigation.

Use Media Queries: As you move to larger screen sizes, use media queries to add styles and features. For example:

CSS

```
@media (min-width: 768px) {
  /* Styles for tablet-sized screens */
}


@media (min-width: 1024px) {
  /* Styles for desktop screens */
}
```

Progressive Enhancement: Gradually add more complex features and layouts as the screen size increases. This ensures that users on smaller devices still have a good experience, while users on larger screens benefit from enhanced features.

Test Thoroughly: Test your website on various devices and screen sizes to ensure it's working as expected. Use browser developer tools and real devices for testing.

Key Takeaways:

Mobile-first is a design approach that prioritizes mobile users.

It offers benefits like improved mobile experience, content prioritization, and performance optimization.

Start with a basic mobile design and progressively enhance for larger screens using media queries.

Focus on content and prioritize essential features for mobile users.

By adopting a mobile-first approach, you can create websites that are optimized for the modern web, providing a great experience for users on all devices. In the next chapter, we'll delve into multimedia, exploring how to incorporate images, videos, and audio into your web pages.

Chapter 8

Working with Multimedia

8.1 Embedding Images and Videos

Adding multimedia elements like images and videos can greatly enhance the visual appeal and engagement of your web pages. HTML provides straightforward ways to embed these elements, bringing your content to life.

Embedding Images

The `<img>` tag is used to embed images in your web page. It requires the `src` attribute to specify the image file's URL or path.

HTML

```
<img     src="images/my-image.jpg"     alt="A
descriptive alt text">
```

`src`: The URL or path to the image file.

`alt`: Provides alternative text that describes the image. This is crucial for accessibility (screen readers) and if the image fails to load.

Tips for Working with Images

File Formats: Use common web-friendly image formats like JPEG, PNG, and GIF.

Optimization: Optimize your images to reduce file size and improve page load speed. Use tools to compress images without sacrificing too much quality.

Responsive Images: Use the `srcset` attribute to provide different image sources for different screen sizes, ensuring optimal display on various devices.

Accessibility: Always provide descriptive alt text for your images, helping users with visual impairments understand the content.

Embedding Videos

The `<video>` element allows you to embed video content directly into your web pages.

HTML

```
<video width="640" height="360" controls>
    <source    src="videos/my-video.mp4"
type="video/mp4">
    <source    src="videos/my-video.webm"
type="video/webm">
  Your  browser  does  not  support  the  video
tag.
</video>
```

`width` **and** `height`: Specify the dimensions of the video player.

`controls`: Adds default video controls (play, pause, volume, etc.).

`<source>`: Specifies different video file formats for compatibility with various browsers.

Fallback content: Provide a message for browsers that don't support the `<video>` tag.

Tips for Working with Videos

File Formats: Use common video formats like MP4 and WebM for broader browser support.

Optimization: Compress your videos to reduce file size and improve loading speed.

Accessibility: Provide captions or transcripts for your videos to make them accessible to users with hearing impairments.

Hosting: Consider using video hosting services like YouTube or Vimeo, especially for larger videos, to offload bandwidth and improve performance.

Key Takeaways:

Use the `<img>` tag to embed images and the `<video>` tag to embed videos.

Optimize your images and videos for web use to improve performance.

Always provide alt text for images and consider captions/transcripts for videos for accessibility.

By incorporating images and videos thoughtfully, you can create more engaging and informative web pages. In the next section, we'll explore how to integrate audio content into your website.

8.2 Audio Integration and Control

Integrating audio into your web pages can create richer and more immersive experiences for your users. Whether it's background music, sound effects, or podcasts, HTML provides the tools you need to seamlessly incorporate audio content.

The <audio> **Element**

The <audio> element is used to embed sound files into your web pages.

HTML

```
<audio controls>
        <source      src="audio/my-audio.mp3"
type="audio/mpeg">
        <source      src="audio/my-audio.ogg"
type="audio/ogg">
    Your browser does not support the audio
element.
</audio>
```

controls: Adds default audio controls (play, pause, volume, etc.).

<source>: Specifies different audio file formats for compatibility with various browsers.

Fallback content: Provide a message for browsers that don't support the <audio> tag.

Attributes for Control

`autoplay`: Starts playing the audio automatically when the page loads.

`loop`: Loops the audio playback.

`muted`: Mutes the audio by default.

`preload`: Specifies how the audio should be loaded (e.g., `auto`, `metadata`, `none`).

JavaScript for Advanced Control

For more advanced audio control, you can use JavaScript to:

Create custom audio players.

Control playback with JavaScript functions (play, pause, stop, seek).

Visualize audio data.

Create interactive audio experiences.

Example: Background Music with JavaScript Control

HTML

```
<audio id="myAudio" loop>

    <source  src="audio/background-music.mp3"
type="audio/mpeg">

</audio>
```

```
<button          onclick="playAudio()">Play
Audio</button>

<button          onclick="pauseAudio()">Pause
Audio</button>


<script>[1]

var x = document.getElementById("myAudio");


function playAudio() {

   x.play();

}


function pauseAudio() {

   x.pause();

}

 </script>[2]
```

This code embeds background music that loops and provides buttons to control playback using JavaScript.

Tips for Working with Audio

File Formats: Use common audio formats like MP3, OGG, and WAV for broader browser support.

Optimization: Compress your audio files to reduce file size and improve loading speed.

Accessibility: Provide transcripts for audio content to make it accessible to users with hearing impairments.

User Experience: Avoid autoplaying audio with sound by default, as it can be disruptive to users. Provide clear controls and allow users to adjust the volume.

Key Takeaways:

Use the `<audio>` element to embed audio files.

Utilize attributes like `autoplay`, `loop`, and `muted` to control audio playback.

JavaScript allows for more advanced audio control and interactivity.

Consider accessibility and user experience when integrating audio.

By carefully integrating and controlling audio content, you can enhance your web pages and create a more immersive and engaging experience for your users. In the next section, we'll discuss accessibility considerations for multimedia, ensuring that your content is usable by everyone.

8.3 Accessibility Considerations

When adding multimedia to your web pages, it's crucial to consider accessibility to ensure that everyone, including people with disabilities, can perceive and understand your content.

Key Accessibility Principles

Perceivable: Information and user interface components must be presentable to users in ways they can perceive.[1] This means providing text alternatives for non-text content, captions for videos, and transcripts for audio.

Operable: User interface components and navigation must be operable. This means ensuring that all functionality is available from a keyboard and that users have enough time to read and use content.

Understandable: Information and the operation of the user interface must be understandable. This means using clear and simple language, avoiding jargon, and providing consistent navigation.

Robust: Content must be robust enough that it can be interpreted reliably by a wide variety of user agents, including assistive technologies. This means using valid HTML and CSS and providing alternative content formats when necessary.

Specific Considerations for Multimedia

Images:

Alt text: Always provide descriptive alt text for images using the `alt` attribute in the `<img>` tag. This text should concisely describe the image content and its purpose.

Decorative images: If an image is purely decorative, use an empty `alt` attribute (`alt=""`) to inform screen readers to ignore it.

Videos:

Captions: Provide captions for all video content to make it accessible to people with hearing impairments. Captions should be synchronized with the audio and include all dialogue and relevant sound effects.

Transcripts: Offer transcripts as an alternative to captions. Transcripts are text versions of the audio content, including dialogue, sound effects, and speaker identification.

Audio descriptions: For videos with important visual information, provide audio descriptions that narrate the visual elements for people who are blind or have low vision.

Audio:

Transcripts: Provide transcripts for all audio content, including podcasts, music with lyrics, and audio recordings. Transcripts should include all spoken words and relevant sound effects.

Controls: Ensure that audio controls are clearly labeled and accessible to keyboard users.

Tools and Resources

WAVE Web Accessibility Evaluation Tool: A browser extension that helps you identify accessibility issues on your web pages.

Web Content Accessibility Guidelines (WCAG): A set of guidelines for making web content more accessible to people with disabilities.[2]

Key Takeaways:

Accessibility is crucial when incorporating multimedia into your web pages.

Provide text alternatives for all non-text content, including images, videos, and audio.

Use captions, transcripts, and audio descriptions to make multimedia content accessible to users with disabilities.

Follow accessibility guidelines and use testing tools to ensure your content is perceivable, operable, understandable, and robust.

By prioritizing accessibility, you create a more inclusive web experience and ensure that your content can be enjoyed by everyone. In the next chapter, we'll move on to CSS frameworks and preprocessors, exploring tools that can streamline your web development workflow.

Chapter 9

CSS Frameworks and Preprocessors

9.1 Introduction to Popular Frameworks (Bootstrap, Tailwind CSS)

CSS frameworks are powerful tools that can significantly speed up your web development process. They provide pre-written CSS code and predefined components that you can easily integrate into your projects, saving you time and effort. Here's an introduction to two of the most popular CSS frameworks: Bootstrap and Tailwind CSS.

Bootstrap: The Front-End Toolkit

Bootstrap is a comprehensive and widely used CSS framework that offers a wide range of pre-designed components, including:

Grid system: A responsive grid system for creating flexible layouts.

Typography: Predefined styles for headings, paragraphs, lists, and more.

Components: Ready-to-use components like buttons, forms, navigation bars, modals, and carousels.

Utilities: Helper classes for styling elements quickly (e.g., spacing, colors, borders).

Getting Started with Bootstrap

Include Bootstrap: You can include Bootstrap in your project by linking to its CSS and JavaScript files from a CDN or by downloading and hosting them yourself.

Use the Grid System: Bootstrap's grid system uses a 12-column layout to create responsive pages. You can define rows and columns using classes like `row`, `col-md-4`, `col-lg-6`, etc.

Utilize Components: Bootstrap provides a wide range of pre-styled components. Simply add the appropriate classes to your HTML elements to use them.

Customize: You can customize Bootstrap's default styles by overriding them with your own CSS rules or by using Sass, a CSS preprocessor.

Tailwind CSS: The Utility-First Framework

Tailwind CSS takes a different approach by providing a vast collection of utility classes that you can directly apply to your HTML elements. This allows for highly customizable designs and avoids the pre-defined look and feel of traditional frameworks.

Getting Started with Tailwind CSS

Install Tailwind: You can install Tailwind using npm, yarn, or a CDN.

Configure: Create a `tailwind.config.js` file to customize the default settings.

Use Utility Classes: Apply utility classes directly to your HTML elements to style them. For example, `p-4` adds padding, `text-blue-500` sets the text color to blue, and `bg-gray-100` sets the background color to gray.

Purge Unused Styles: Tailwind's build process removes unused styles to keep your CSS files small and efficient.

Choosing Between Bootstrap and Tailwind CSS

Bootstrap: Ideal for rapid prototyping and projects that benefit from pre-designed components. It offers a faster initial setup and a familiar structure.

Tailwind CSS: Ideal for highly customized designs and projects where you want complete control over the styling. It can lead to smaller CSS files and improved performance.

Key Takeaways:

CSS frameworks provide pre-written CSS code and components to speed up development.

Bootstrap offers a comprehensive set of components and a responsive grid system.

Tailwind CSS provides utility classes for highly customizable designs.

Choose the framework that best suits your project's needs and your preferred development style.

By utilizing CSS frameworks, you can streamline your workflow and create visually appealing and responsive websites more efficiently. In the next section, we'll explore CSS preprocessors, another powerful tool for enhancing your CSS development process.

9.2 Using CSS Preprocessors (Sass, Less)

CSS preprocessors take your styling capabilities to the next level. They are scripting languages that extend the functionality of CSS, allowing you to write cleaner, more maintainable, and more powerful stylesheets. Sass and Less are two of the most popular CSS preprocessors.

Benefits of CSS Preprocessors

Variables: Store values like colors, font sizes, and spacing in variables, making it easy to reuse them throughout your stylesheets. This promotes consistency and makes it easier to update your styles.

Nesting: Nest CSS rules to reflect the structure of your HTML, improving code organization and readability.

Mixins: Create reusable blocks of code for common styles, reducing repetition and promoting DRY (Don't Repeat Yourself) principles.

Functions: Use built-in functions or create your own to perform calculations and manipulate values within your CSS.

Code Organization: Import and split your CSS into multiple files, improving organization and maintainability for larger projects.

Sass (Syntactically Awesome StyleSheets)

Sass is a mature and feature-rich CSS preprocessor with two syntax options:

SCSS (Sassy CSS): Uses a CSS-like syntax with curly braces and semicolons.

Indented Syntax: Uses indentation to define code blocks, making it more concise but potentially less familiar to those used to traditional CSS.

Example (SCSS):

```scss
$primary-color: #007bff;

.button {
  background-color: $primary-color;
  color: white;
  padding: 10px 20px;
}
```

Less (Leaner Style Sheets)

Less is another popular CSS preprocessor with a syntax that closely resembles regular CSS. It's generally considered easier to learn for beginners.

Example:

```less
@primary-color: #007bff;

.button {
  background-color: @primary-color;
  color: white;
  padding: 10px 20px;
}
```

Using a CSS Preprocessor

Choose a Preprocessor: Select either Sass or Less based on your preferences and project needs.

Install a Compiler: You'll need a compiler to convert your preprocessor code into regular CSS. Many tools are available, including command-line tools, GUI applications, and task runners.

Write Your Styles: Write your stylesheets using the syntax of your chosen preprocessor, taking advantage of features like variables, nesting, mixins, and functions.

Compile to CSS: Use your compiler to convert your preprocessor code into regular CSS that can be used in your web pages.

Key Takeaways:

CSS preprocessors extend the functionality of CSS with features like variables, nesting, mixins, and functions.

Sass and Less are two popular CSS preprocessors with slightly different syntaxes.

Using a preprocessor can improve code organization, maintainability, and efficiency.

You'll need a compiler to convert your preprocessor code into regular CSS.

By incorporating CSS preprocessors into your workflow, you can write cleaner, more powerful, and more maintainable CSS code, ultimately enhancing your web development process. In the next chapter, we'll focus on debugging and optimization techniques to ensure your websites are error-free and performant.

9.3 Streamlining Your Workflow

CSS frameworks and preprocessors are valuable tools, but there are even more ways to streamline your web development workflow and boost productivity. Here are some key strategies and tools to help you work smarter, not harder:

1. Task Runners and Build Tools

Task runners like **Gulp** and **Grunt** automate repetitive tasks, such as:

CSS preprocessing: Compiling Sass or Less files into CSS.

Minification: Reducing the size of CSS and JavaScript files for faster loading.

Code concatenation: Combining multiple files into a single file to reduce HTTP requests.

Image optimization: Compressing images to improve page load speed.

Live reloading: Automatically refreshing the browser when you save changes to your files.

2. Version Control Systems

Version control systems like **Git** are essential for tracking changes to your code, collaborating with others, and reverting to previous versions if needed. Popular platforms like **GitHub**, **GitLab**, and **Bitbucket** provide hosting and collaboration features.

3. Code Editors and IDEs

Choose a code editor or IDE (Integrated Development Environment) that suits your needs and offers features like:

Syntax highlighting: Color-coding your code for improved readability.

Autocompletion: Suggesting code completions to speed up typing.

Error detection: Identifying potential errors in your code.

Debugging tools: Helping you find and fix bugs in your code.

Extensions and plugins: Adding functionality to your editor, such as linters, formatters, and Git integration.

Popular choices include **VS Code**, **Sublime Text**, **Atom**, and **WebStorm**.

4. Browser Developer Tools

Modern web browsers have powerful developer tools that help you:

Inspect HTML and CSS: Examine the structure and styles of your web pages.

Debug JavaScript: Step through your code, set breakpoints, and inspect variables.

Analyze network activity: Monitor HTTP requests and identify performance bottlenecks.

Test responsiveness: Simulate different screen sizes and devices.

5. Design and Prototyping Tools

Design tools like **Figma**, **Sketch**, and **Adobe XD** help you create visual mockups and prototypes before writing code. This can improve communication with clients and stakeholders and ensure a smoother development process.

6. Collaboration and Communication

Effective collaboration and communication are essential for efficient workflows. Use tools like **Slack**, **Microsoft Teams**, or **Google Chat** for team communication, and project management tools like **Trello**, **Asana**, or **Jira** to keep track of tasks and progress.

Key Takeaways:

Task runners automate repetitive tasks and improve efficiency.

Version control systems are essential for tracking changes and collaborating.

Choose a code editor with features that enhance your workflow.

Utilize browser developer tools for debugging and testing.

Design tools help you create visual mockups and prototypes.

Effective communication and collaboration are crucial for smooth workflows.

By incorporating these strategies and tools into your web development process, you can streamline your workflow, reduce errors, and boost productivity. In the next chapter, we'll focus on debugging and optimization techniques to ensure your websites are error-free and performant.

Chapter 10

Debugging and Optimization

10.1 Common HTML and CSS Errors

Even experienced web developers make mistakes! HTML and CSS errors can lead to unexpected behavior, broken layouts, and a frustrating user experience. Here are some common errors to watch out for:

HTML Errors

Typos in Tags and Attributes:

Misspelling tag names (e.g., `<p>` vs. `<p >` or `<div>` vs. `<divv>`)

Incorrect attribute names (e.g., `scr` instead of `src` for images)

Case sensitivity issues (e.g., `<Img>` instead of `<img>`)

Missing Closing Tags:

Forgetting to close tags like `<div>`, `<p>`, or `<tr>` can disrupt the structure of your page.

Unclosed or Mismatched Tags:

Having an opening tag without a corresponding closing tag or vice versa.

Nesting tags incorrectly (e.g., `<p><strong>This is bold</p></strong>`).

Incorrect Nesting:

Placing elements in the wrong order (e.g., putting a `<div>` inside a `<p>`).

Missing or Incorrect DOCTYPE:

Not including the `<!DOCTYPE html>` declaration or using an outdated version can cause rendering issues.

Invalid Attribute Values:

Using incorrect values for attributes (e.g., `color="bleu"` instead of `color="blue"`).

Missing Alt Text for Images:

Forgetting to provide alt text for images using the `alt` attribute in the `<img>` tag.

CSS Errors

Typos in Property Names and Values:

Misspelling property names (e.g., `clor` instead of `color`).

Using incorrect values (e.g., `text-align: center` missing the semicolon).

Missing Semicolons:

Forgetting to add semicolons at the end of declarations.

Incorrect Selectors:

Using incorrect syntax for selectors (e.g., `.class#id` instead of `.class #id`).

Misplaced Curly Braces:

Not opening or closing curly braces correctly in rule sets.

Conflicting Styles:

Having multiple styles that conflict with each other, leading to unexpected results. (Understanding CSS specificity is important here.)

Overusing `!important`:

Relying too heavily on `!important` can make your CSS harder to maintain and debug.

Tips for Avoiding Errors

Use a Code Editor with Validation: Code editors like VS Code can help identify errors as you type.

Validate Your Code: Use online validators like the W3C Markup Validation Service to check your HTML and CSS for errors.

Test Thoroughly: Test your website in different browsers and on different devices to catch any issues.

Use Browser Developer Tools: Inspect your code and identify errors using the developer tools in your web browser.

Keep Your Code Organized: Use proper indentation and comments to make your code easier to read and debug.

By being mindful of these common errors and using tools and techniques to catch them early, you can create cleaner, more reliable, and more maintainable web pages. In the next section, we'll explore how to use browser developer tools to debug your code effectively.

10.2 Using Browser Developer Tools

Modern web browsers come equipped with powerful developer tools that are essential for debugging and optimizing your web pages. These tools provide a deep dive into the inner workings of your website, allowing you to inspect HTML and CSS, analyze JavaScript, track network activity, and much more.

Accessing Developer Tools

Most browsers provide similar ways to access their developer tools:

Right-click: Right-click anywhere on a web page and select "Inspect" or "Inspect Element."

Keyboard shortcuts:

Chrome & Edge: Ctrl + Shift + I (Windows) or Cmd + Option + I (Mac)

Firefox: Ctrl + Shift + I or F12

Browser menu: Look for "Developer Tools" or "Web Developer Tools" in the browser's menu.

Key Features of Developer Tools

Elements Panel (Inspector):

Inspect HTML: View the HTML structure of the page, including the DOM (Document Object Model) tree.

Edit HTML and CSS: Make live changes to the HTML and CSS to see how they affect the page in real-time.

Analyze styles: Inspect the CSS styles applied to any element, including computed styles, inherited styles, and CSS rules.

Console Panel:

View logs and errors: See JavaScript logs, errors, and warnings.

Execute JavaScript: Run JavaScript code in the context of the current page.

Debug JavaScript: Set breakpoints, step through code, and inspect variables.

Network Panel:

Monitor network requests: Track all HTTP requests made by the page, including their status, timing, and content.

Analyze performance: Identify potential bottlenecks and optimize page load speed.

Sources Panel:

View page resources: See all the files loaded by the page, including HTML, CSS, JavaScript, and images.

Debug JavaScript: Set breakpoints and step through your JavaScript code.

Performance Panel:

Analyze page performance: Record and analyze performance metrics like page load time, rendering time, and memory usage.

Identify performance issues: Find areas for improvement and optimize your website's speed.

Tips for Using Developer Tools Effectively

Inspect Element: Right-click on any element on the page and select "Inspect" to quickly jump to its HTML in the Elements panel.

Live Edit CSS: Make changes to CSS properties in the Elements panel to see their effect instantly.

Use the Console: Use `console.log()` in your JavaScript code to print values and debug your scripts.

Analyze Network Activity: Identify slow-loading resources and optimize them to improve page load speed.

Simulate Mobile Devices: Use the device emulation feature to test how your website looks and behaves on different screen sizes and devices.

Key Takeaways:

Browser developer tools are essential for debugging, testing, and optimizing web pages.

Use the Elements panel to inspect and edit HTML and CSS.

Use the Console panel to view logs, execute JavaScript, and debug your code.

Use the Network panel to monitor network requests and analyze performance.

Utilize the various features of developer tools to improve the quality and performance of your websites.

By mastering browser developer tools, you can become a more efficient and effective web developer, creating websites that are both visually appealing and technically sound. In the next section, we'll discuss techniques for optimizing your websites for performance and accessibility.

10.3 Optimizing for Performance and Accessibility

Creating websites that are both fast and accessible is crucial for providing a positive user experience. Performance optimization ensures that your pages load quickly and smoothly, while accessibility ensures that everyone, including people with disabilities, can perceive and interact with your content.

Performance Optimization

Optimize Images:

Compress images: Reduce file sizes without sacrificing too much quality using tools like TinyPNG or ImageOptim.

Use appropriate formats: Choose the right image format (JPEG, PNG, GIF, WebP) based on the image content.

Use responsive images: Serve different image sizes for different screen sizes using the `srcset` attribute or picture element.

Lazy load images: Load images only when they are about to be displayed in the viewport.

Optimize Code:

Minify CSS and JavaScript: Remove unnecessary characters (whitespace, comments) from your code to reduce file sizes.

Concatenate files: Combine multiple CSS and JavaScript files into a single file to reduce HTTP requests.

Remove unused code: Eliminate any CSS or JavaScript that is not being used on the page.

Improve Server Response Time:

Choose a fast web host: Select a hosting provider that offers good performance and server response times.

Use a CDN: Utilize a Content Delivery Network (CDN) to distribute your website's assets across multiple servers around the world.

Cache static assets: Configure your server to cache static assets (images, CSS, JavaScript) to reduce server load.

Minimize HTTP Requests:

Combine images into sprites: Combine multiple small images into a single image and use CSS to display specific sections.

Use CSS instead of images: Use CSS to create visual effects whenever possible instead of relying on images.

Reduce the number of external resources: Minimize the use of external scripts and stylesheets.

Accessibility Optimization

Semantic HTML: Use appropriate HTML elements to structure your content (e.g., headings, lists, tables) and provide semantic meaning.

ARIA Attributes: Use ARIA (Accessible Rich Internet Applications) attributes to provide additional information to assistive technologies[1] (e.g., `aria-label`, `aria-describedby`, `role`).

Keyboard Accessibility: Ensure that all interactive elements (links, buttons, forms) are accessible using the keyboard.

Color Contrast: Use sufficient color contrast between text and background to ensure readability for users with low vision.

Alternative Text for Images: Provide descriptive alt text for all images using the `alt` attribute.

Captions and Transcripts for Multimedia: Provide captions for videos and transcripts for audio content.

Tools for Optimization

Lighthouse: An open-source tool that audits web pages for performance, accessibility, best practices, and SEO.

PageSpeed Insights: A Google tool that analyzes web page performance and provides suggestions for improvement.

WAVE Web Accessibility Evaluation Tool: A browser extension that helps identify accessibility issues.

Key Takeaways:

Optimizing for performance and accessibility is crucial for a positive user experience.

Performance optimization techniques include optimizing images, code, and server response time.

Accessibility optimization involves using semantic HTML, ARIA attributes, keyboard accessibility, and sufficient color contrast.

Utilize tools like Lighthouse, PageSpeed Insights, and WAVE to analyze and improve your website's performance and accessibility.

By prioritizing performance and accessibility, you can create websites that are fast, inclusive, and enjoyable for everyone.